Dolin

Routledge & Kegan Paul

London and Henley

Dolin

FRIENDS AND MEMORIES

Compiled by Andrew Wheatcroft

Foreword by
Dame Ninette de Valois

First published in 1982 by Routledge & Kegan Paul Ltd
39 Store Street, London WC1E 7DD, Broadway House,
Newtown Road, Henley-on-Thames, Oxon RG9 1EN
Set in Monophoto Gill Sans 262
and printed in Great Britain by
BAS Printers Ltd., Over Wallop, Hampshire

ISBN 0 7100 9199 0

Dedicated to
Her Majesty Queen Elizabeth the Queen Mother

CONTENTS

PREFACE

Working with historic images is usually a solitary pursuit, carried out in archives and collections filled with the shadows of people long dead and places much altered. I therefore looked upon the idea of working with Anton Dolin, very much *in vivo*, with a nervous anticipation. The intention of this preface is to explain how we prepared this book and why it takes the form it does.

The first principle we have worked with is that it is *his* book, and not mine. Every picture has been taken from his own collection, every word either in his own handwriting or produced in conversation. Despite my fears, the creation of the book has been an entirely delightful process and I have been struck by his capacity to remember people, places and events with uncanny precision. My contribution has been to take the many thousands of images, stuffed into albums, cupboards, drawers and boxes, and to form an evocation of the many aspects of his life. Throughout his life and career, Anton Dolin has taken risks, followed his own inclinations rather than the path of convention. This book, like his life, is in a sense experimental. There is no lapidary text, no assessment of The Life, or The Career. It is a set of episodes, of friends and memories, with coherence given to it by the facts and events of his life, and the development of dance in our century. Indeed, at many points, the two are synonymous.

I would also like to express my thanks to a small number of people. First, and most of all, to Anton Dolin himself, whose friendship I now prize very dearly. It was Kaori O'Connor who originally had the inspiration for this book, and I am grateful to her both for the idea and for her infectious enthusiasm for the project. Turning to the content, a book of photographs always involves much skilled work in processing poor and fugitive images. All the work for this book has been carried out by Philip de Bay and Ken Jackson, of Images, 83 Hazlebury Road, London, SW6. It is thanks to their expert treatment of both negatives and prints that the quality of many of the copies is superior to that of the originals in their present state. The fine design by Jo Hart has done much to enhance them and I am grateful to him.

One other hand has gone into the creation of the book. My wife, Janet, and I have been through all the images together, discussed which should be included and which rejected, and how the book should be presented. Her knowledge of the period, and of the world of theatre and dance is much superior to mine, and without her work, the book would have taken a different, and I believe, less satisfactory form.

Andrew Wheatcroft

FOREWORD

The history of ballet in the twentieth century will undoubtedly place on record that Anton Dolin was the first British male dancer to receive both national and international recognition. It could be argued that he was fortunate – for competition in the 1920s, concerning the position of male dancers in England, was not at its peak. He was further exceedingly fortunate to be engaged by the Diaghilev Company – along with his little student companion, Alicia Markova. But he held his position, as a distinguished dancer in this country and elsewhere, alongside the ascendence of such male dancers as Robert Helpmann, Walter Gore, Harold Turner and Michael Somes, for all these talented artists had emerged by the early 1930s.

In those days of the mid-1920s his dancing brought a spark of virility to the male classical dance picture. It was Madame Nijinska who first brought out his particular virtuoso form of attack; it had nothing in common with the purer form of accepted classical virtuosity; it was an advent that foretold a development of male classicism in the 1920s. His style was considered, at that time, to be verging on the athletic. His work invariably had an athletic quality about it, and this approach, in certain roles, made him more of an athletic dancer than a character dancer.

Apart from his career as an individual – covering character roles as well as classical – he inspired confidence in his partners. He always said how much he loved this side of his work, but he did not have to stress the obvious, for we were all aware of his interest in this direction when dancing with him.

I have appeared in a revue with him, in divertissement at the Coliseum, and recitals in the provinces. But what I most enjoyed was choreographing for him – not that it was his habit to give me much time to work with him! The most important role I mounted on him was Satan in Vaughan Williams' *JOB*. This role was performed by him when *JOB* was first produced for the Camargo Society just fifty years ago; a little later the ballet was transferred to the Sadlers Wells repertoire. He also reappeared in it, many years later, when it was revived at Covent Garden after the war.

I say that I 'choreographed' the role of Satan on him, but I actually had to create it on a young member of the Sadlers Wells Company as Dolin could not give me more than three rehearsals. Yet perhaps he never had a role that suited him better: I must have had a very clear picture of him in my mind when working it out on a young dancer of little theatre experience, but who resembled Dolin physically. I remember prompting Dolin all through the dress rehearsal; those were tough demanding days that would not be tolerated in these times. It is a fact that I found myself using his athletic style in any work that I created for him. It is curious, but worth noting, that, on the whole, Dolin's response to a woman choreographer was more sympathetic and rewarding than his approach to a male choreographer.

For some years after Dolin left the Diaghilev Company he was a freelance dancer. During this period he made many appearances – sometimes for some weeks on end – with the young Vic-Wells Ballet in the early 1930s. He often partnered Markova (the permanent ballerina of the company for some years) until they both left in 1935 to form their own company.

As a young man Dolin was a law unto himself and this he has remained. Hardly possible for him to do otherwise. Born Patrick Healey-Kay, Pat is, although a British subject, the complete and absolute Irishman. It is a state of affairs that stresses, forever and a day, the land that he belongs to – and I sincerely hope that Ireland is justly proud of him – for he has worn his Dublin dancing shoes with the same buoyant bravura that 'J.R.' bestows on his Dallas stetson.

Dame Ninette de Valois

INTRODUCTION

I have had so far a long, exciting and, at times, frustrating life. I have travelled the world – everywhere except China. Travelled, not always first class, but quite comfortable tourist. Today airports have become increasingly exasperating and exhausting. Once on the plane, fine, but the everlasting lining-up, the security, being knocked to pieces by other people's hand-baggage, takes the joy out of travelling. Especially when so often my journeys are alone, though sustained by the thought of friends I shall see on arrival, whatever my destination.

This book of photographs and memories, alas too often of friends I have no longer at my calling, has been a nostalgic delve into my past. In my apartment is a huge collection of photographs, cupboards and drawers full of them, with posters, cuttings, letters – what Andrew Wheatcroft calls 'my archive'. I don't know how I collected it all, but this book has grown from what I have hoarded and collected over the years.

The book goes back beyond Christmas 1916, when I knew my first beloved friend of the theatre, Ellaline Terriss, or 'Bluebellaline' as Lady Hicks preferred to be called. My first professional job – £2 a week, twelve shows a week – was as Peter, The Black Cat. I have always regarded it as a good omen, for with the Irish half of me, I am very superstitious. It was a lovely Christmas play, *Bluebell in Fairyland*. How much I learned during the rehearsals and the three months of performances from Sir Seymour Hicks, a wonderful, kind man.

I have from the beginning of my career known the greats of my professions. I say professions because, though perhaps best known as a ballet dancer, I have truly been of the Theatre, and very nearly once, of the Circus. I have been lucky because, having given, I have had much given to me – love, affection, and the most valuable of all, friendship.

It has not always been an easy passage. Believe me, I have suffered the pangs of disappointment, the heartbreak of unrequited love and the sadness of death. But still I can sit in my home, long shared with a true friend, John Gilpin, and talk with dancers about ideas, projects, plans for the future. Thank God that life is ahead and not left behind.

I write these words in December 1980. My mind though is concentrated on 1981. For that reason I find it difficult to concentrate on the last remaining days of this year. I want in every way to forget it. A letter and the 40th anniversary of my beloved American Ballet Theatre were my only true moments of joy in 1980. The rest was anxiety, sadness and desperate worry. But I am not the only one.

This is a book of friends. Inevitably many will be left out, but certainly not forgotten. Life has been long, eventful. I repeat myself. Why not? Honesty and saying what I felt and meant has always been my most stupid, but most relished, accomplishment. I hate, detest, the understatement of accomplishment. A star is a star.

Someone whom I respect as a writer and to whom I showed what I had written, felt it was rather defeatist and not my usual self. 'It should be full of happiness,' he said, 'and show your wonderful zest for life.' I do not want it to be a defeatist treatise. Far from it. I am thrilled with life, but at 76 one has to think about what might lie ahead. And in all normal conditions it does not give much time.

There will be, I feel sure, omissions in this book of photographs. Much as I would like, it is not possible to include everyone I love and have known. For, if anyone was blessed with friends, I have been. So there must be something good about me, with all my faults which I am told about on many occasions. I do not mind.

This year of 1981, as I write these few last words, I go to Buckingham Palace with two beloved friends as my guests: Alicia Markova, DBE and John Gilpin, the great English dancer. I go to receive from our beloved Queen Elizabeth II the accolade of a Knight of the British Empire.

I am happy, proud to sign these most inadequate words.

Sir Anton Dolin

Me, by Rankin, 1926. I gave the picture to Lady Campell-Orde

My father, H. G. Kay. He died in 1921, handsome and still with blue-black hair. From the look on his face, he obviously was not too happy at me, Paddy, wishing to be a *ballet* dancer

My mother, 1914

IN THE BEGINNING

This is where I was born on 27 July, 1904. It used to be called Ashby Cottage, but now it is called Dolphins, so eliminate 'ph' and it is Dolins

With my brothers: Anthony in his sailor suit and Philip in his uniform, 1917

School: I moved, of course, so my face is blurred

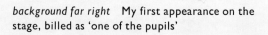

Peter, The Black Cat, 1916, at the Prince's Theatre, aged 12½. This was my first job, at £2 a week

background far right   My first appearance on the stage, billed as 'one of the pupils'

THEATRE ROYAL,

WORTHING.

Grand Matinee

ARRANGED BY

MISS FLORENCE GODDARD

— ON —

Saturday, Dec. 4th, at 2.30.

PROCEEDS FOR

BELGIAN REFUGEES FUND.

Accompanist: Miss FLORENCE GODDARD.

Piano kindly lent by Mrs. SCOTT, South Street.

Programme, Twopence,

Observer Co., Printers, Worthing.

above left   This is me as John, in *Peter Pan*, aged 14

above right   Me as David Playne in *Betty*, Dalys Theatre Tour, 1917. It was probably one of the best touring companies ever sent on the road. Adrienne Brune, then Billie Brown, was Betty, Miles Clifton played G. P. Huntley's old part and Walter Passmore the one created by W. H. Berry. I played David, one of the best parts for a boy ever written in a musical comedy.

The tour started at Scarborough and having no idea that rooms should be engaged beforehand or even how to set about finding them once we had arrived in the town, my mother and I stayed in a hotel far too expensive for the salary of £5 a week I was earning

Me as Dick, in *The Man Who Knew The Future*

Gaby Delys, whom I idolised, 1917. I think the pearls
were a little gift from a King of Portugal

My first photograph as a dancer – bewitched,
bothered and bewildered, 1916. I still am in 1981

Madame Seraphine Astafieva, my teacher, 1919.
Night after night I would sit up with one or two
other pupils listening to the tales Astafieva would
tell us of Russia – the school and the dancers, then
almost a legend to me but many of whom I was later
to know so well. Many times in the evening I would
get an old pair of toe shoes from the dressing-room,
put them on and, with Astafieva singing the music,
dance all the solos from *The Sleeping Princess*.

  How happy those days were! Each morning at
class something new to learn, something beautiful to
do. Sometimes we had no pianist and then she would
sing or chant in a rich typically Russian voice and
beat time with a long jewelled stick. What
personality she had! A short dark dress to the knees,
always white stockings covering her beautifully
formed legs, little pink ballet slippers or else the
extreme – black shoes with heels so high that it used
to puzzle me how she managed to walk on them let
alone show us the steps before we were to do them.
Her head always swathed in a coloured silk bandeau,
ropes of pearls, long finger nails, perfectly shaped
hands, always a cigarette in her mouth. That is how I
remember her

Fedora programme, 1917. This was the last time I appeared as Patrick Kay. The performance was given at the Globe Theatre with Marie Lohr, Ellis Jeffreys, Allan Aynesworth, Henry Vibart and Basil Rathbone in the cast. I played the comparatively small but quite important part of the Russian page – important in so far as certain lines I had to say had a bearing on the situation upon which the play was written.

At one of the early rehearsals, Sir Squire Bancroft, who came in to watch and, I believe, supervise one or two details, spoke to me and told me to go over my lines. He asked me whether I spoke French, and I told him I did not. Then he asked me to pronounce the word '*Madame*' with a French intonation. Upon hearing it he said, 'No, my lad, you'd better say it in English. Don't try to speak like a Frenchman.'

right To Seraphine Astafieva I owe my association with the Russian Ballet. The first time I ever saw her was at the London Coliseum in August 1917, when she was appearing in her production of the Swinburne Ballet. As usual, I was with my mother, and although the story has been told before in various interviews, it is quite true that I turned to her and remarked: 'I will and must learn to dance in her school.' Nothing would satisfy me, and I did not rest until she took me to see Astafieva and arranged that I should study with her.

That it was to be the first really serious move in my dancing career and the result it was to have only she knew, for I honestly think that the moment Astafieva saw me do a few steps she foresaw everything that was to happen – everything!

I had my first lesson on 24 August, 1917, and I turned up in a pair of brown velvet knickers and a Little Lord Fauntleroy coat to match, thick woollen socks and black shoes.

How dreadful I must have looked!

Every Evening at 8.30

FÉDORA

by

VICTORIEN SARDOU

Count Loris Ipanoff	BASIL RATHBONE
Jean de Siriex	ALLAN AYNESWORTH
Pierre Boroff	WILLIAM STACK
Dr. Loreck	ALFRED GRAY
Gretch	HENRY VIBART
Boleslav Lasinski	LINDON LANG
Tchileff	A. CARLAW GRAND
Desiré	E. VIVIAN REYNOLDS
Dmitri	PATRICK KAY
	(By arrangement with Italia Conti)
Kirill (*The Coachman*)	DRELINCOURT ODLUM
Boris (*The Porter*)	CHARLES BISHOP
Ivan	E. A. WALKER
Basil (*Servant to Fedora*)	REX CALDWELL
Princess Fédora Romazova	MARIE LÖHR
Countess Olga Soukareva	ELLIS JEFFREYS
Marka (*Maid to Fedora*)	M. BALVAIRD HEWETT

The Play produced by LOUIS N. PARKER

Synopsis of Scenery

ACT I. Count Vladimir's Study Russia
ACT II. Reception Room in the House of the Countess Soukareva Paris
ACT III.—Princess Fédora's House Paris
ACT IV. The Same

Scenery painted by JOSEPH & PHIL. HARKER

Orchestra under the Direction of CARLTON MASON

Programme of Music

1	Song, "None but the Weary Heart"	*Tchaikovsky*
2	From Foreign Parts	*Moszkowski*
3	Hindu Song	*Rimsky-Korsakov*
4	(a) The Swan (b) Dance Macabre	*Saint Saens*
5	Operatic Fantasias Changed at each Performance	
6	Malaguena	*Moszkowski*
7	Invitation to the Dance	*Weber*
8	Prelude, "Le Déluge"	*Saint Saens*
9	Fantasia, Reminiscences of Grieg	
10	Fantasia on Russian Folk Tunes	
11	(a) Petite Suite (b) "Children's Corner"	*Debussy*
12	Suite, "Othello"	*Coleridge-Taylor*

Miss Marie Lohr's Dresses by WORTH
Miss Ellis Jeffreys' Dresses by HANDLEY SEYMOUR
Other Dresses and Costumes by B. J. SIMMONS & Co., and Miss LEVERICK
Wigs by CLARKSON
Objets d'Art kindly lent by ERNEST RENTON
Furniture by BAILEY'S, Ltd., High Street, Kensington

Matinées—Every Wednesday and Saturday at 2.30

Stage Manager, E. VIVIAN REYNOLDS
Assistant Stage Manager E. A. WALKER
Acting Manager and Treasurer, J. J. MOORE
General Manager .. .. **HENRY DANA**

The Box Office is Open from 10 to 9.30 Daily. Telephone: Gerrard 8722

PRICES OF ADMISSION
Private Boxes £3 3 0 and £1 11 6 Stalls 10 6 Dress Circle 10 6 and 7 6
Upper Circle 5 - Pit 2 6 Gallery 1 -
The above Prices are Exclusive of Entertainment Tax

Ladies are earnestly requested to remove Hats, Bonnets, or any kind of Head-dress. This rule is framed for the benefit of the Audience, and the Management trusts that it will appeal to everyone, and that Ladies will kindly assist in having it carried out.

The Theatre is so well provided with Exits, that every member of the Audience can without hurry, get clear of the Auditorium within TWO MINUTES.

THE NEAREST TUBE STATIONS TO THIS THEATRE ARE PICCADILLY CIRCUS AND LEICESTER SQUARE.

Extracts from the Rules made by the Lord Chamberlain

For my little
"Pattka"
Nastatra

DIAGHILEV AND DOLIN

inset 1920: One of my teachers,
the great Russian, Nicholas Legat,
always used to call me 'Piccadilly',
saying he thought I looked like
'Eros' in Piccadilly Circus. Perhaps
he was right

inset One night, during the run of *The Sleeping Princess* in 1921, as I was watching Stanilas Idzikowski and Lydia Lopokova dancing *The Blue Bird*, from the side of the stage, Diaghilev came up to me practically for the first time since I had been in the company. Putting his arm on my shoulder, he remarked: 'And when will you dance *The Blue Bird*?

'When you want me to, Sir,' I replied immediately.

The first time I danced *The Blue Bird* in London, he sent me a laurel wreath and on his card, attached to it, was written: 'Quand dancerez-vous L'Oiseau Bleu?' 1921–4

A class with Bronislava Nijinska, London, 1921, before the rehearsal for *The Sleeping Beauty*, Drill Hall, Chenies Street. That's me with the handkerchief over my hair.

At the end of one of those rehearsals the following incident happened: Diaghilev, who was sitting next to Leon Bakst in the stalls watching a rehearsal, suddenly turned to him and asked: 'What are the three most beautiful things in this theatre today?'

'Olga Spessiva, the little boy with the big brown eyes, and me.'

I was 'the little boy with the big brown eyes'.

I did not know this story at the time, of course, but it was told to me by Olga Spessiva later.

How I loved her! She used to call me 'Little boy with the shawl' for always I would wait in the wings for her as she made her exit and place a covering round her delicate shoulders.

I don't think I missed once, during the whole of the run of *The Sleeping Princess* in London, watching from the wings, when I was not actually engaged on the stage, Spessiva or any of the other famous dancers Diaghilev had engaged for this revival of Petipa's marvellous ballet. I recall every movement and different interpretation that each one of them gave to the same *adagios*, the same solos and *codas* that occurred in each of the acts of the ballet. Where Spessiva was so perfect in one, Vera Trefilova was equally so in another and Lubov Egorova in still a different one

left Madame Kschessinska, by marriage a Romanov, and a princess of the ballet – *prima ballerina assoluta*

On the way to Monte Carlo, 7 November, 1923. The next day I left Paris at eight o'clock and after travelling all night arrived at Marseilles. The journey from there, along the marvellous sea coast and red rock that abounded everywhere, was a series of beautiful pictures. Cannes, Nice, Antibes – all places I had read of but had never seen – now loomed before me. Finally Monte Carlo, where I expected to see a large imposing station. Instead, I alighted at what seemed so insignificant, almost suburban, a station for the important place I knew Monte Carlo to be. A small boy screaming 'Ascenseur' was the first sound I heard on arrival. A porter took my luggage to a cab which conveyed it and me to my hotel.

It was Friday early in the afternoon when I arrived. I had expected it to be hot, but although the sun was shining, I was far from warm. I went out after dinner and walked around. Passing by the Café de Paris, I saw Lydia Sokolova and Leon Woizikowsky drinking coffee. Being practically the only members of the company I knew at all well, I wanted to go and talk to them but did not do so, deciding to wait until we should meet on the Monday.

Saturday and Sunday were two of the loneliest days I have ever spent in my life. I should have been thrilled and excited at my new surroundings but I was not. I could not speak French and I knew no one.

Sunday night I dined with Diaghilev. He talked to me about the work I was to do and how I was to conduct myself at lessons and rehearsals. He emphasised the necessity of being particularly attentive to Nijinska, who was not too pleased at my appearance in the company, and how, once on my side and reconciled to the idea of my being there, she could help me more than anyone. She had three young pupils who had been in her school in Kiev – one of them was Serge Lifar – who had just arrived in the company. At the audition in Paris she told Diaghilev that she saw no reason for my being engaged, as she considered there was quite enough young talent to be brought into the limelight without engaging anyone else, and particularly a foreigner who would need so much coaching and preparing before he would finally be ready to step into the many roles that were then waiting to be filled

inset left   Boris Kochno, Serge Pavlovich de
Diaghilev and Picasso Jnr, outside the Hotel de Paris,
Monte Carlo, January 1924.

I could not help noticing that Diaghilev was
displaying a certain lack of interest in his company
and in the work that was being done. On some days
he would not even trouble to come down, but used
to send Kochno. I know he had perfect confidence in
him but it was not the same thing. His hair which, up
till then, had been so marked by a characteristic
white streak that went through it, was now
becoming uniform in its greyness and the white
streak was no longer so apparent.

Little did we know it was the beginning of the
end. Poor Serge Pavlovich! Though he must have
been so ill he told no one. Perhaps it was his illness
that made him so much kinder and more tolerant of
his artists.

I remember sitting watching him light a
rehearsal. Picture an empty theatre save for two or
three people in the stalls: one young, good-looking –
Boris; the other, Diaghilev, a large being enveloped
in a huge fur coat, the only part of his body to be
seen, an enormous head with two eyes that peer out,
kindly at one moment, fierce as a raging fire the
next. The stage is set – it is dark. One realises that
there is some scenery there, not quite discernible
but with a strange beauty about it, even in this
lighting. 'Le directeur' sits and watches and dictates
– sometimes in a tone almost too gentle for a
woman, sometimes too fierce for a man. His
commands are 'hurled' at the stage: 'There, there is
too much light. Here, there is not enough. More
blue above, more green' and so on.

To light one scene Diaghilev would spend
hours. I have known him sit in a theatre from ten
o'clock in the morning until two-thirty in the
afternoon and even then not finish lighting it to that
perfection which was his fetish – never tired, always
watching, watching, watching!

inset right   Lubov Tchernicheva and Vera Nemchinova
amid the Battle of the Flowers in Monte Carlo, 1924

background   What grace, what style . . . Monte Carlo

Cecchetti as Cecchetti, Monte Carlo, 1925

Me as Cecchetti, in the Herbert Ross film, *Nijinsky*,
1979. They said many nice things about me

inset left Hamburg, 1924. The 'little boy with the big brown eyes', but now well launched on his career

above Isadora Duncan. I met her in November 1924. We were together in the lift at the Hotel Eden, Berlin. She looked at me with her great, childish, but wicked, eyes, and remarked, 'You are Anton Dolin: you are much too handsome to be an *acrobat*.'

Evidently she had seen *Le Train Bleu* the day before, and never having seen me dance any other role but this one, thought I was not a classical dancer which would have been her desire. I met her at lunch the following day when she was full of her plans for the future – The Temple of the Dance, as she referred to it then and all through her life.

The last time I saw her was in Nice not long before her death. I am glad she died when she did – not too old to destroy entirely the atmosphere of beauty she had created during her lifetime

background Me, holding a newspaper, with Serge Diaghilev and Boris Kochno, Hamburg, 1924

DIAGHILEV AND DOLIN

Vaslav Nijinsky, Paris, 1924, with his second daughter, Tamara, aged 4.

Nijinsky has always been to me a legendary inspiration. I never saw him dance, but any work of merit in my career with the Russian Ballet was inspired first by the man I had never known and then by the haunting memory of someone I had seen more in a vision than as a living person. During my first season in Monte Carlo, I asked Diaghilev to arrange for me to see him and he promised that he would.

Before I realised the desire of my life – a meeting with this genius of the dance – I remember an incident that stands out as a sheer contrast. One afternoon I went with some friends to a Chanel dress parade. I have been bored many times but somehow never quite so bored as on this occasion. My one wish in life was to meet someone who, I thought had worn clothes far finer and more magnificent than any mannequin of Chanel's could ever hope to display.

About two days later I saw Diaghilev, who told me he had telephoned Madame Nijinska and had arranged that we were to go to tea that afternoon. How the day dragged on. The taxi drive seemed interminable. Eventually we arrived at our destination. Facing us was a block of grey granite flats; I do not remember the address: my French at that time was very imperfect and I failed to observe it. All I remember is going up in a lift three or four flights and knocking at a door which was opened by a short Russian manservant about 30 years of age. The large door was swung open. We entered the hall, our hats were taken and we were shown into the drawing-room. There, sitting in front of us, like a convalescent invalid, was the greatest of all dancers – my inspiration – the man on whom I had built all my ideas, the man whose achievements had always spurred me on in life.

His wife greeted us. I was presented to her. Hardly a word was spoken, but somehow in this man's face there was something more expressive than a volume of words. There were the same eyes I had seen in pictures, the same beautiful mouth, the upper lip clean-shaven and dark, hardly any hair on the head at all, white hands that were never still.

This was Nijinsky!

All around the room were portraits. I distinctly remember Sargent's famous painting of the great dancer. There were various photographs, flowers in the window, lace curtains – it was almost suburban . . . and then, above a desk, a doctor's chart recording the varying temperatures of the invalid.

Diaghilev tried to make him speak. He wouldn't say one word. He just sat and laughed. I asked him something and he answered 'Je ne sais pas.' Four words that expressed the whole tragedy – he didn't know.

Altogether we were there for sixty minutes. It seemed like sixty days. It was and ever will remain the happiest and most tragic moment of my life.

I found Madame Nijinska, who spoke a little French, most charming. Their little daughter came in, a pretty child, a really lovely child.

I often wonder what Diaghilev's feelings were; whatever they were he succeeded in hiding them. During tea Nijinsky would not eat or drink. He seemed powerless to do anything. He looked as healthy as any of us, yet somehow his brain refused to work. He sat in his chair trying to understand. I believe he did understand a great deal but I think his brain was tired.

At last we rose to go. Diaghilev embraced him. By this time I was feeling the strain of the meeting and could hardly hold out my hand to say goodbye. I put my arms on his shoulders. Perhaps it was my fancy but he seemed to resent it. After a moment, however, he lifted up his hand and, placing it on my shoulders, kissed me on the cheek three times as all Russians do on leaving. He came to the door with us, said goodbye in Russian and then, when Diaghilev asked if we should come again, nodded his head in a wistful way as much as to say: 'I am very, very tired.'

above Five Enchanted Princesses, with their Bluebird, at the London Coliseum, 1924. They were all different sizes and weights, so it's no wonder I became a good partner. *Front row* Ludmilla Schollar, Vera Savina, Alice Nikitina. *Back row* Felia Dubrovska, Alexandra Danilova

right I talked to Coco Chanel, a few months before her death. She had no idea at first who I was. In almost impeccable French, I said, 'I am Dolin. The only man you ever dressed.' 'Nonsense, cher Dolin', she replied, 'I never *dressed* a man in my life.'

far right Le Train Bleu, the ballet that brought me fame. But only because of the other four in the photograph, Lydia Sokolova, Jean Cocteau (who wrote it for me), Leon Woizikowsky and Bronislava Nijinska, who choreographed the 'Operetta Danse' as Serge Diaghilev named it. The sculptor, Henri Laurens, designed the decor, the costumes were designed and made by Coco Chanel.

All through the opening night of the ballet I was in a trance, hypnotised. Everywhere in front of me were eyes – eyes. One paper said I walked on air. Perhaps that night I did. Nothing seemed to hurt me. My body for that half hour did not belong to me. Someone other than myself, someone far greater, had taken control of it and those senses were telling it what to do. It was not then to feel the cuts and bruises it was sustaining. It had to leap from a spring board at the side of the stage. Sometimes it would be more than six feet in the air and then fall on to its knees. How it never smashed all its bones I do not know.

The curtain was lowered and raised countless times, and through a haze I began to realise and hear the audience crying 'Dolin! Dolin!'

The stage by now was a mass of laurels and flowers. Nobody knew who most of them were for. What did it matter? They were for the Russian Ballet, of course

NERMAN

Nerman's view of me in *Le Train Bleu*. He did this in 1924

The Terrace, Monte Carlo, March, 1925. I know it was March 'cos I had just got my new 'plus fours' from Nice and was not allowed through the main entrance to the casino or opera house. With me are Alicia Markova, aged 14, and Michel Pavlov, in whose apartment in New York I found this photograph in October, 1980

Darling Bea Lillie gave me this photo in 1925. She gave me more, year by year

66,GLEBE PLAC[E]

CHELSEA, S[...]

KENSINGTON[...]

Atcha! I just thought I'd call to see what you [were] up to. Also to see if you had anything to eat !! Atcha you naughty little [...]

B

MIDLAND HOTEL BIRMINGHAM

TELEGRAPHIC ADDRESS: "NEAREST, BIRMINGHAM."

BIRMINGHAM.

TELEPHONES:
2600 MIDLAND (8 Lines).
2604 Do. MANAGER.

Tuesday.

Dear little Atcha

Many thanks for your letter. I haven't had a chance to write to you as we are rehearsing every moment [...] the show every night [...] marvellous notices [...] I don't think much of [...] being a good girl [...] child. [...]

WESTERN CABLE

THE WESTERN UNION TELEGRAPH COMPANY. ANGLO[-]

RECEIVED AT 22, GREAT WINCHESTER STREET, LON[DON]

3PZ FJE 1541   STLOUIS MO [...] 17

561
WLT ANTON DOLIN   BLUE COTTAGE CRANLEY M[...]

THANKS FOR LETTER DEAR LITTLE AT[CHA]

No. of Telegram   Office Stamp

WESTRA'D
25 OCT 25

Received here at

[...] 22=50

= ANTON DOLIN VAUDEVILLE THEATRE STRAND LONDON

FAREWELL PAT BE GOOD AND DONT FORG[ET]

SHOW[...]

UNION
ABLEGRAM
LC
NLT
Ship
HONED TELEGRAM
1945 SEP 24 AM 8
ION
AM
TELEGRAPH Co. LD
(Tel. No. London
1926 APR 19
NSINGTON LOND
VE
BEATRICE
C
attended to witho
UCCESS LOVE
BEATRICE

below   Anna Pavlova. I took Beatrice Lillie, Lydia
Sokolova and Serge Lifar to see Anna Pavlova dance
at Streatham the last time but one that she appeared
in London.

To say that she was greater than ever is not
true, but to say that she was still the supreme
mistress of her art, is. It seemed uncanny to watch
the years suddenly leave her as she danced
Snowflakes, one of her favourite ballets and also that
of her adoring public. Bad scenery, costumes that
were hardly worthy of a second-class pantomime,
music that was often uninteresting – all these – but
when Pavlova was on the stage and danced, the whole
took on a new light.

Though certain technical feats may have been
slowed down in their *tempo* of execution her
amazing balance only seemed to gain in power. I
wonder how many people know that to balance on
one toe alone without a partner to hold her for
seemingly endless periods as Pavlova did, is one of the

most difficult feats it is possible to accomplish. I have only seen one other dancer with the same balance – Trefilova.

After the matinée we all went round to see her; and whereas on the stage dancing she seemed so tall, so strong, one could hardly recognise the great artiste in this tiny little person with her flashing black eyes, as we crossed to greet her. She talked to us for a few minutes and for the first time she and I spoke to each other in Russian. 'Where was I dancing?' 'Was I happy?'

'I hope you will come and see me again to talk for a long time,' she said. 'Now I must go for there is another peformance. I must sleep and eat.'

'Au revoir, Madame.'

'Au revoir, Serge. Au revoir, Dolin. À bientôt.'

below   *Le Spectre de la Rose*, Diaghilev Ballet. I danced it for the first time in the Opera House, Monte Carlo, in January, 1925. The costume was once worn by Nijinsky. Maestro Cecchetti said 'pas mal'

Jessie Matthews. I am of the opinion that had Jessie cared to devote herself to dancing alone she would have been a perfect dancer of the classical school, as even in 1926 she was one of the finest dancers of her type in revue or musical comedy

A rare photograph of me only because I am smiling, but I *was* looking at Jessie. London, 1926

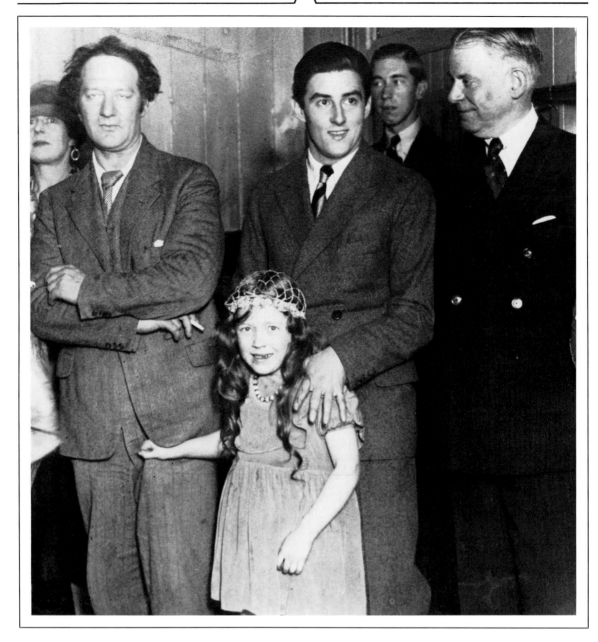

A party in 1926, with Kay Banfield, Jacob Epstein with his little daughter, me, Richard Adinsell, and C.B. Cochran

Toasting Jacob Epstein's famous models, Sunita and Dolores. 1926

Dancing on a carpet! A charity performance, or something, at the Royal Albert Hall, 1927. The floor was too slippery.

But four years before I had made my first appearance under my new name, Anton Dolin, at the Albert Hall on 26 June, 1923. As a part of my contribution to the programme I wanted to dance *The Hymn to the Sun* and *Danse Russe*, both of which I had arranged myself. Quite naturally Astafieva wanted the whole entertainment to be of her choice, and at first she would not agree to my selection.

Then I displayed both temper and temperament for the first time in my life. I screamed and raved and said that if I were not allowed to dance these numbers, I would not appear at all. But Astafieva seemed to understand, for instead of stifling and suffocating these feelings she allowed them to have full play.

I have done much finer work since, but never have I had such unanimous praise from the critics. Monica Ewer, writing in the *Daily Herald* of 26 June, 1923 said: 'One does not expect to find anything outstanding at a casual dancing exhibition. Yet last night, at the Albert Hall, among the Princess Astafieva's ballet, was a young man in advance of many of the established stars of to-day. That young man is Anton Dolin. He combined the most marvellous agility with a true dramatic instinct. He does one particular jump which I have never seen attempted before. But – more important – the feeling which he puts into his work triumphed over the extraordinarily inappropriate surroundings of the Albert Hall. When I am old I hope to say condescendingly: "The great Dolin? I saw him dance when he was an unknown lad!"'

The good life in Le Touquet, Juan les Pins and
Antibes

DIAGHILEV AND DOLIN

The Rhapsody in Blue. The final moment as I lay in the arms of my English Corps de Ballet, London Coliseum, 1927. The first ever choreographic realisation of George Gershwin's great music, and a great success, even if I say it myself, 'cos I did it.

The idea of staging a ballet for George Gershwin's 'Rhapsody in Blue,' came to me quite suddenly. I had first heard the music at a party given by Mrs Mathias at which Diaghilev and I had been the guests of honour.

There had been some talk once of Gershwin writing a ballet for Diaghilev and although I tried to get him interested in the idea it had failed to materialise. I have never been able to understand why he disliked, or said he disliked, Gershwin's music; it was brilliantly rhythmical and should have appealed in some form or other to his dancing brain.

All the best work I have done in my life has been inspired by something or somebody; this was to be no exception. It took me seven days to produce *The Rhapsody in Blue*. I based the idea of my ballet on the music which, to me, expressed the antagonism of jazz against the classical element of life. Jazz remains one of the many expressions of modern life. In producing it, I in no way forgot the technique on which ballet stood for all these years, but with this ground work I tried to eliminate graceful poses and curves which would have been out of sympathy with the atmosphere I was trying to create. I had to introduce angles and straight lines which helped to express the modern thought

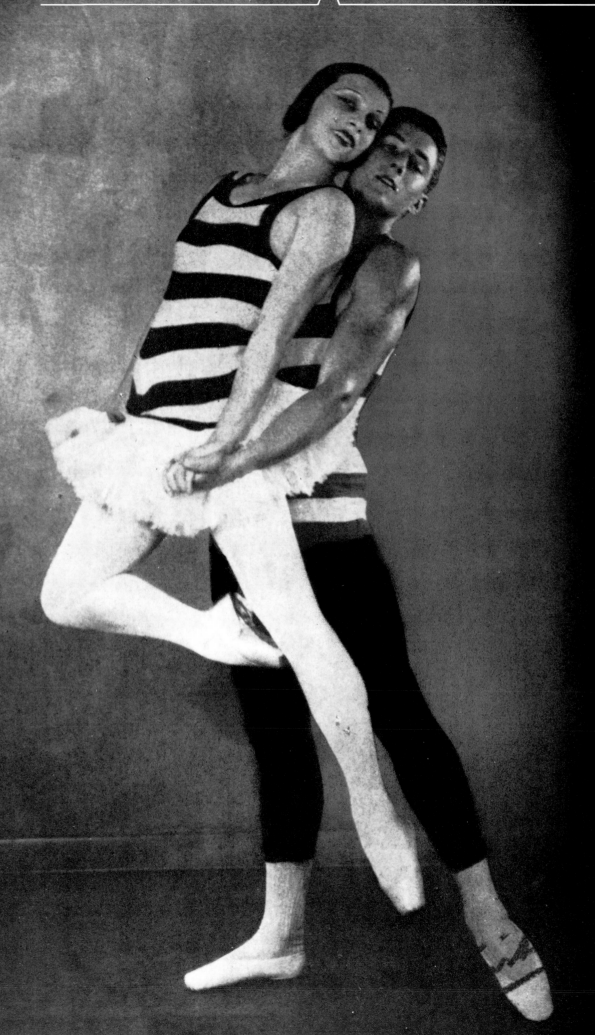

In a Classroom. The music was Satie (*Gymnopédies*), the choreography mine, the lovely dancer in my arms, Vera Nemchinova. The stage we first danced it upon was the London Coliseum, 1927–8.

Although Nemchinova and I had danced together a great deal in the Russian Ballet, and there had become so used to each other as partners, the time that had elapsed since those days made us appear as complete strangers to each other when we first started to rehearse. Every ballerina has a different way of preparing to do a pirouette. While one likes to be held beforehand, another cannot turn at all if she feels her partner's hand on her waist. Karsavina hardly held her partner's hand when she danced; Pavlova even less; Nemchinova liked to feel a strong hold on her hand before doing a particular *adagio* movement.

That first rehearsal did not end with either of us very happy at the thought that within six days we should have to appear together again before a critical audience. All the next morning and afternoon, with no break even for lunch, was spent in rehearsing and gradually once more we began to 'find' ourselves.

By Thursday evening, when I recalled the company, Nemchinova practically knew her role in *The Nightingale and the Rose* as well as the first *pas de deux* we were doing. This I had danced once before with Phyllis Bedells at a charity matinée and it meant simply showing her the steps as I had previously arranged them; thus with only one or two slight alterations it remained the same, I called it *In a Classroom*, the idea being that two dancers stroll into a studio, go through the fundamental exercises of their work and then nonchalantly walk out at the end. The simplicity of it added greatly to its popularity. We were dressed in practice clothes just as though we were about to have a lesson, she wearing a white ballet dress with a yellow vest on top; I in black tights with a black and yellow tunic

Tamara Karsavina

right Although she could hardly see, she inscribed her name and mine, 4 April, 1978. This photo of Karsavina in *Spectre de la Rose* was taken in 1927.

Lunching one day at the Savoy I had happened to say to Mr Wollheim, who was there, how much I had always wanted to dance with Karsavina. He was her manager and had a few weeks previously arranged a contract for her at the London Coliseum, which unfortunately terminated after the first performance owing to an accident to her foot. She had now practically recovered and was to take up her engagement in three or four weeks' time. At that moment she had no partner. Here was the opportune moment and two days later it was arranged that I should dance with her.

We decided to revive Fokine's ballet, *Spectre de la Rose*. It had not been danced in London for some considerable time and Karsavina's role in it would not be too great a strain on her leg, which, although well enough to dance on, was not yet very strong. Her part was not really a tiring one, although only she has really brought out to the full extent the beauty of this choreographic masterpiece. To dance one performance of *Spectre de la Rose* is a strain, but to dance it twice a day, as I did at the Coliseum, was something that I only undertook because of Karsavina and because it meant the fulfilment of an ambition

I called her 'Shadow', she called me 'Dreamer'. Her
name was Desha. 1928–80

For old times sake — 1928 - 1959 To my favourite dancer Pat Do... from ...

left   Dancing with Anna Ludmilla, London, 1929. Also a brief nuptial engagement of three months

above   The line is good. It should be, in 1927

WENDY TOYE

Phyllis Strickland   Vera Harris
Eileen Baker   Anita Verdi
Guy Massey   Fred Franklin

and

ANTON DOLIN

ORCHESTRA SPECIALLY AUGMENTED FROM LONDON

SARA ALLGOOD
JOAN FRED EMNEY

, 8th OCTOBER 1934

Nightly at 8.15

inees : Wed. & Sat. at 2.30

PANY

OLIN

ET

The Rhapsody in Blue: Vera Nemchinova and me, London Coliseum, 1928. Our partnership was proving a complete success in every way.

During this season Nemchinova and I used to dash over to Covent Garden to see Pavlova whenever the opportunity occurred. She seemed to be dancing more brilliantly than ever. I remember after the last performance which I attended, I went round to see her in her dressing-room. Although the evening had been long and trying, she was the freshest of them all. The members of the audience who had been applauding and calling her again and again to the footlights were tired, but the reason for their exertions was like a strange flower that never drooped its petals nor ever closed when the sun did not shine. I reminded her of the student she had seen at Legat's studio. 'Mais oui,' she replied, 'mais nous sommes toujours les élèves, n'est ce pas?'

Between shows at the London Coliseum, 1929: Anna Ludmilla, Arthur Crocker, me and Margaret Bannerman, for once without her toque. Alas, she is no longer with us, but who will ever forget her in Somerset Maugham's *Our Betters*

Boy, what an officer! *Le Bal*, 1929   *right*   The most beautiful woman I ever knew, Marcelle Chantal, 1928

Serge Diaghilev in Venice

It was during the filming of *Dark Red Roses* that the tragic news of Diaghilev's death came to me. I was sitting alone in the garden of the film studio waiting to be photographed. A man came round with the evening papers. I called him over and bought one. As I opened it I saw a small photograph of Diaghilev on the front page. Without reading I knew what it meant. My heart left me for a moment and I floated in space. I do not faint or ever show much emotion over death, but this was so sudden and dramatic. Crying 'Serge Pavlovich est mort' I dashed over to where Lopokova and Balanchine were sitting.

Poor Lydia! Poor George! Poor artists of the Russian Ballet!

How sad we were. Tears rose up in our eyes and a quietness came over everything. In the distance I heard him call again: 'Quand danserez vous *L'Oiseau Bleu*?'

Lopokova kept on saying: 'Big Serge, poor poor Big Serge. He was so tired, so very tired. But he died in Venice, Pat, think of that. Oh God, how good of Him to Big Serge.'

Diaghilev had always expressed a desire that the end should come in Venice. His wish was granted.

On the evening of 18 August, 1929 he became unconscious, and passed away just before the dawn of the next morning; he lies in the cemetery of San Michele in the Venice which he loved so dearly

Vichy, August, 1929. Last days of the Diaghilev
Ballet. Me, with Natalia Branitska and Serge Lifar

At Diaghilev's tomb, San Michele, Venice; Igor
Kosak (my adopted son), Carl Musil and me, 1968

DIAGHILEV AND DOLIN

Mae West might have said 'Come up and see me sometime.' 1928

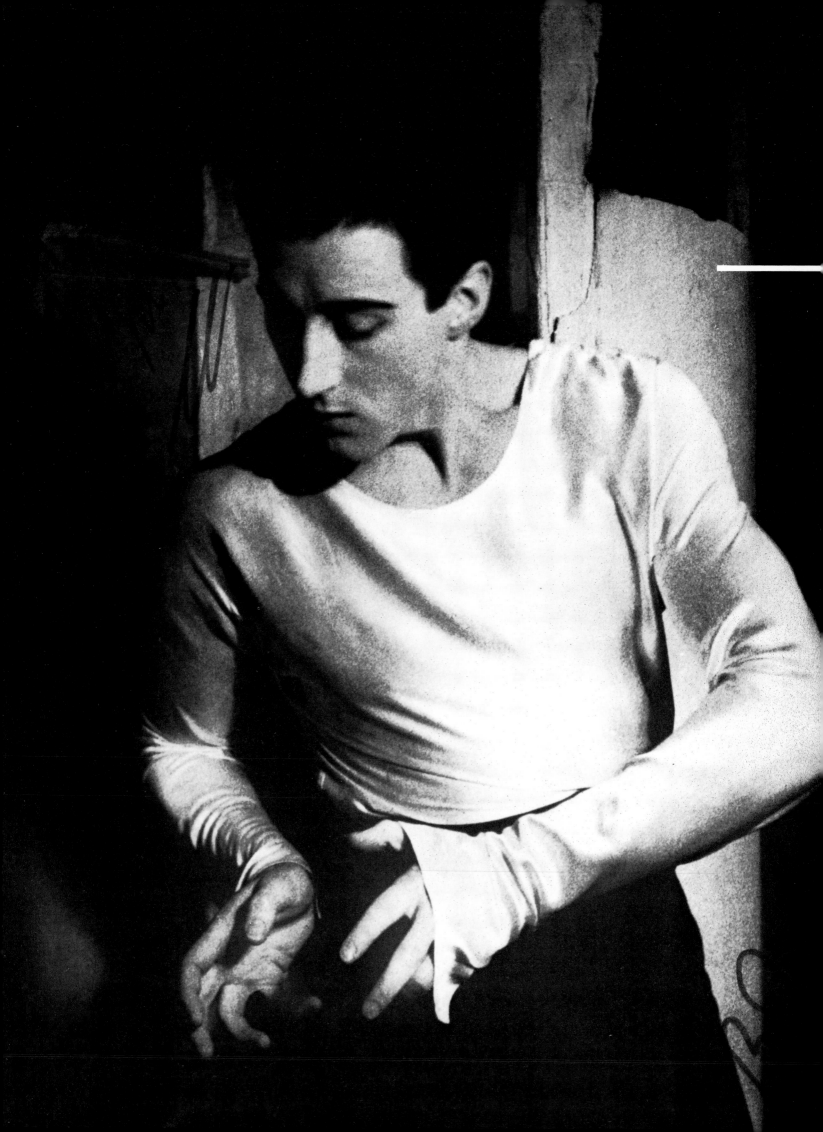

BALLET
GO ROUND

The Tales of Hoffmann, the Doll Ballet, Berlin, 1931.
Alex von Swaine, Maria Solveg. Looking on – Tamara
Desni, Nina Theilade and Brigitta.

Max Reinhardt was the most difficult person I
have ever worked for, perhaps because of the fact
that I did not, at that time, understand or speak the
German language as I do now. That certainly was a
handicap as Reinhardt's wishes and orders had to be
given through a third and, very often, a fourth
person. Frequently his instructions were not always
translated to me as perhaps he wished. I got them in
a very confused kind of way. It was only later that I
realised that Reinhardt himself had a very confused
way of discussing and thinking about the dance.

Never in all my experience have I known so
many people with their own little axes to grind and
favours to ask. Each day brought something new:
'Do give Fraulein So-and-so something outstanding
to dance in the Doll Ballet.' This one wanted
something. That one wanted something else. From
the publicity department to the stage director's
office and back to the management someone had
someone 'who would like to be favoured'.

Like a fool, I listened and tried to do my best.
The result – the Doll Ballet – was awful and had to
be done all over again; this time I listened to no one
and used them all *en masse*, with no little bits of solo
work thrown in, to please someone with influence.

But Reinhardt's production of *The Tales of
Hoffmann* had some unforgettable moments of sheer
beauty. The Venetian scene with the brilliant
technical use of the revolving stage was a memorable
one; the gondolas going in different directions,
timed to a second; the one arriving at the Palazza
gates just as the last notes of the famous *Barcarolle*
were sung was a perfect piece of stagecraft, achieved
with that artistry that only Reinhardt possesses; the
costumes by Professor Schewrich, the orchestra of
eighty under the baton of Leo Blech, the assembling
of such opera stars as Jarmila Novotna, Friedel
Schuster, Tatjana Menotti, and Carl Hauss, and
actors like Paul Graetz, Vladimir Sokolov, and
Baclanikov made a combination that only a
Reinhardt could conceive

above With lovely Tilly Losch, our only dance together at the Austrian Embassy, London, 1930, for one of Baron Franckenstein's renowned fancy dress parties

right She called me 'Dolinchin', she was La Jana. Berlin, 1931–2

She was certainly one of the most beautiful creatures I have ever set my eyes on, with a figure, though almost boyish in its slightness, that was something at which to wonder. In the strict sense of the word she could not dance. But could she move? Like a gazelle!

Back bend and on my toes.
Berlin, 1931

BALLET GO ROUND

A Cecil Beaton costume and me in it. *Charlot's Masquerade*, Cambridge Theatre, London, 1931

Job, Satan flung from heaven, full of bruises. I consider the Camargo Society's most important contribution to ballet was the first presentation, on 5 July, 1931, of *Job*, Blake's vision of the Book of Job, invented by Geoffrey Keynes, with music by Vaughan Williams, and produced by Ninette de Valois. I portrayed the role of Satan. *Job* was an enormous success, and both the ballet and I received a wonderful press.

The *Dancing Times* said: 'Anton Dolin, as Satan, was superb. Red-haired, talon-handed, his muscular body naked but for a loin cloth, he was the personification of the Fiend as pictured by Blake, and his leaps, his gestures, and his demoniacal expression all served to further enhance his characterisation of the part. His challenge to Heaven, his usurpation of the Throne, and his terrific fall from on high, when ejected by the angels, were magnificent movements and provided the most impressive moments of the ballet.'

I'm sure I must have known I was being photographed. 66 Glebe Place, Chelsea, SW3, 1931

With the most beloved of friends, Adeline Genee. This is her farewell performance at the Royal Theatre, Copenhagen, 1932

Left One of the most happy of engagements, *Stand up and Sing*. I stood up and sang and danced for fifteen months at the London Hippodrome, with Jack Buchanan, Elsie Randolf, Vera Pearce and Anna Neagle. 1930–1

right 'Butterflies and Roses'. Adeline Genee gave the miniature to me in 1948 – a treasured possession

BALLET GO ROUND

inset left   My third change of make-up for the final scene of *David*, performed at the Duke of York Theatre, London, 1935

inset right   My make-up for the third and fourth scenes. Tamara Karsavina came to see *David* and told me that it was 'beautiful and God fearing'

The final scene of a fine ballet: *David* choreographed by Keith Lester and first performed on 11 November, 1935 in Newcastle. It shows David's dance before the Ark

BALLET GO ROUND

Jenny Dolly, a star

BALLET GO ROUND

I called her 'Gink', her other name is Lilian Harvey. 1935.
    I began by giving Lilian dancing lessons, and fell madly in love with
her the first time I straightened her leg in an *arabesque* in a studio off
Sloane Street. We went round London together, driving in her large car,
a huge big cream thing, one of the most conspicuous in which I have ever
driven. It drew a lot of attention wherever we went, and often, when we
came out of the studio after a lesson, or from having lunch at Scott's
Restaurant, we had literally to fight our way through the crowd which
had assembled and were standing gaping at it.
    Lilian wasn't in love with me. We were very good friends though,
and I think she liked me. Perhaps she never knew how much I really
adored her. I don't think I ever told her

BALLET GO ROUND

Alicia Markova, me, Diana Gould and Prudence
Hyman, at Haslington Hall, 1936

For years I have collected photographs of the 'man we have lost', King Edward VIII. Molly Stanford gave me this photo in 1960, inscribed 'for always' – the writing is HRH's

I was there. Just behind the photographer. Staying, as I was, at Jane O'Malley's villa at Biarritz, and having just had, and won, two sets of tennis from HRH Prince George. Lovely days. August 1932

This is another from my collection, a present from Mary and Bill Liefe, 1977

My mother and me at our St Anne's, Blackpool home, during my stint at the Opera House. I was appearing in a revue co-starring Elizabeth Welch, Stanley Holloway and George Lacy. More happy days in 1938 before flying off to Australia

My 33rd birthday party at 66 Glebe Place, Chelsea (wish I had it still).
Left to right   Oliver Messell, Godfrey Winn (sitting), Lydia Sokolova (standing next to me), and at the piano, Alicia Markova, Larry Adler and Doris Barry

My mother again

My birthday party again.
Left to right   My mother, Phyllis Bedells, lovely Mrs Cohen, Murray Anderson, Helen McGuinness, me and a cigarette, and Leighton Lucas

Yes, it *is* a good photograph, by Gordon
Anthony, London, 1938, of me in *Spectre*. It was
taken just before I flew to Australia

right With my only star pupil, Belita, rehearsing
in the Hotel du Cap, Antibes, 1936

far right With Belita at the Salle Pleyel, dancing the
pas de deux in the *Bluebird*, 1938

With Margot Fonteyn at the matinee I organised in 1937 for Nijinsky at His Majesty's Theatre. It put £3,000 into the bank and helped pay the bills that Romola (his wife) acknowledged to me by letter, but not in her books.

Although her lovely face is hardly shown in the photo, there is no mistaking who it is. Margot danced, and danced beautifully, the *Aurora pas de deux* with me, and Maude Lloyd replaced Markova in *Bar aux Folies Bergère*. Mary Honer and Harold Turner performed the *adagio* from *Casse Noisette*. Serge appeared in *L'Après-midi d'un Faune*. Molly Lake, Diana Gould, Prudence Hyman, and Kathleen Crofton danced in the *pas de quatre* arranged by Keith Lester, and finally Lydia Sokolova and my small pupil, Belita Jepson-Turner, making a debut, completed the dancing programme. Martinelli sang in honour of Nijinsky.

The most beautiful moment of all came when Karsavina spoke at the close of the afternoon. At my request she had come to London from Budapest, making the journey specially for the occasion. Lovely Karsavina, there have been few prouder moments in my life than this one when, with privilege and honour, I brought you from the wings to speak your few so well-chosen words about your one-time dancing partner, whose triumphs you had shared and for whom, in his hour of sickness, you had come to express your deep sympathy and understanding

inset How proud I was when Bronislava Nijinska
gave me this and signed it 'Always with love Bronia'.
1937

Nijinsky matinee, with Tamara Karsavina. Here I am leading a great lady forward, to pay her tribute to Vaslav Nijinsky

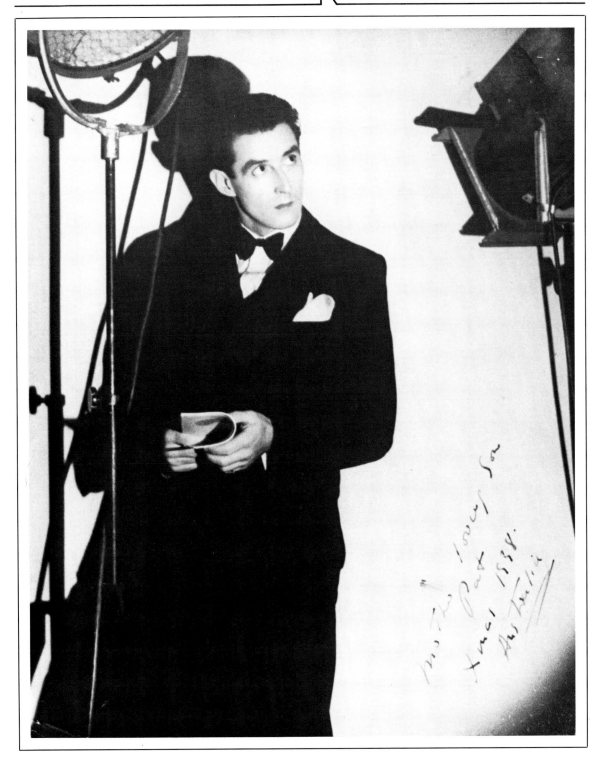

left   Me as The Prodigal Son. Ballet choreographed
by David Lichine, Melbourne, Australia, 1938

above   Australia, 1938. God, how handsome you are,
Mr Dolin!

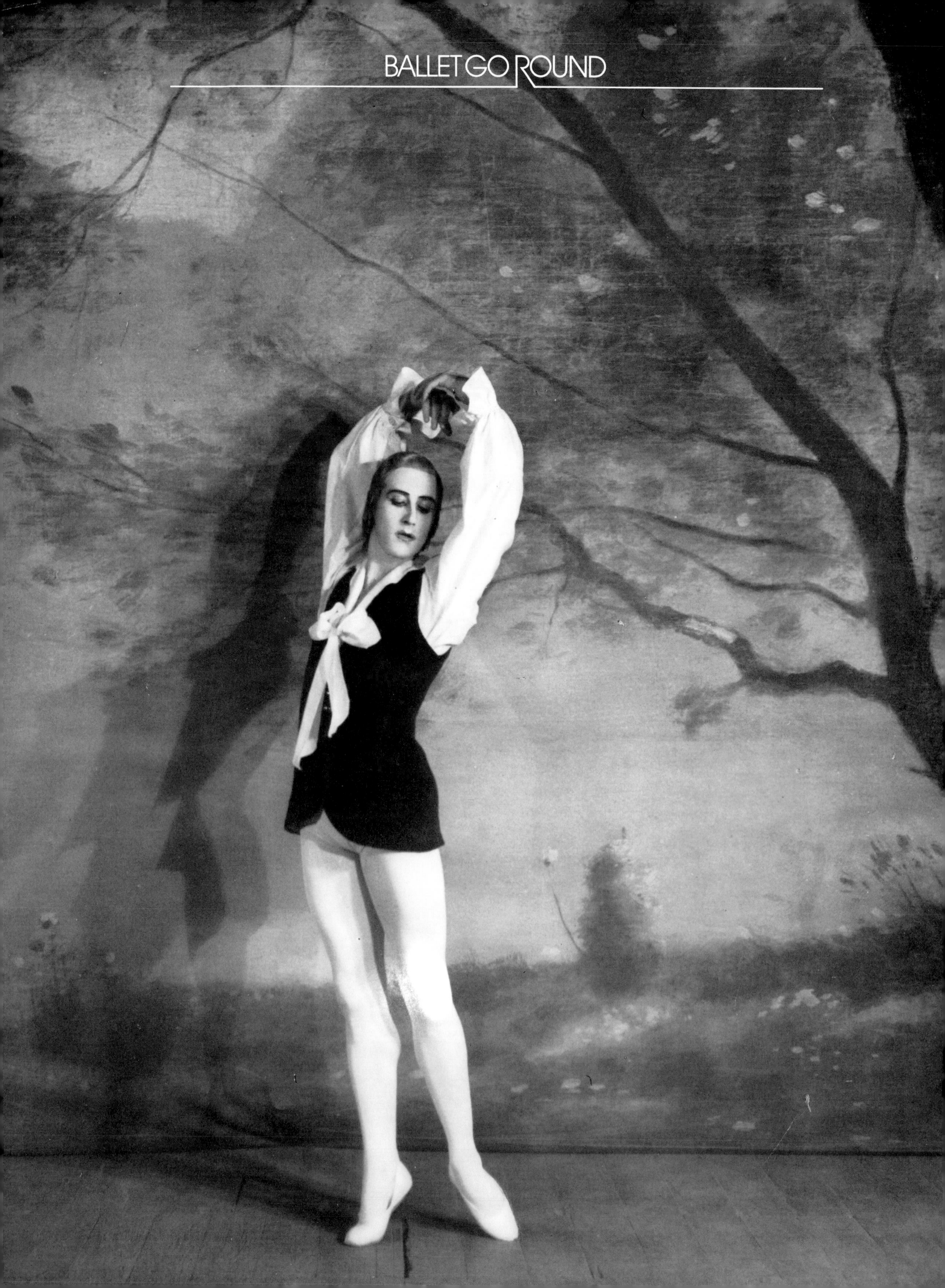

left A damn good study in a ballet I never really enjoyed dancing, *Les Sylphides*, performed in Wellington, New Zealand, 1939

above Irina Baronova – a beautiful Odette and a joy to partner

THE
GREAT WHITE
WAY

Lovely Annabel Lyon, my first Giselle, in New York, January, 1940

above   Sol Huroks' house warming party, Beverly Hills, California, with handsome Otis Pierce, Ethel Barrymore, Alicia Markova and me. My eyes were bad, obviously

left   'Here's looking at you, kid.' Well, it was in Hollywood in the 1940s

right   Olga Spessiva drew this in New York in 1940

below Taglioni and the Scotsman, or Markova and Dolin, a lovely *pas de deux*. That earned a lot of dollars in America for war relief. 1940–5

Quite a party in New Orleans!
Left to right Alicia Markova, John Kriza, Simon Semonov, Lucia Chase – look where her hand is on the handsome sailor's leg – William Skipper (the handsome sailor) and me

Me as Bluebeard: who wouldn't
have a twinkle in his eye with
these three lovelies around him,
my darling Irina Baronova, Mimi
Gomber and Margaret Banks. 1942

The 1942 film of *Pas de Quatre*, with Alicia Markova, Nora Kaye, Annabel Lyon, and me. Here, Nora Kaye, with me kissing her hand.

We made a film – for free – for the Mexican Red Cross, but it was lost on the way to New York

Gosh, how different we looked then, Montreal,
Canada, 1942. Yes, it *is* Hughie Green

A very dear friend, a great actress and a real star,
Greer Garson, Hollywood, 1943

Three *beautiful* men in a garden near Mexico. The
other two are David Nillo and Johnny Kriza. 1942

Constantin

Maurice Seymour

25

inset above   On my toes again, as the Red Devil in David Lichine's ballet *The Fair at Zorochint*, American Ballet Theatre, 1944

inset left   *Don Domingo*, 1943 in Mexico, Massine's amusing Mexican ballet for American Ballet Theatre

Bluebeard, Fokine's ballet and a happy one for me, American Ballet Theatre, Metropolitan Opera House, New York, 1943. Alicia Markova, me in the middle, and Lucia Chase

left 'The Black Pearl' of the ballet, the beauty
Tamara Toumanova, dancing in *Giselle*, act I, 1944

above Encarna Argentinita loved this photograph,
as I do; it's opening night at the Metropolitan Opera
House, New York, 1944

After *Pas de Quatre*, Los Angeles, 1945. What a star-studded group it is —
Nora Kaye, Rosella Hightower, me, Lilian Harvey, Nana Gollner,
Annabelle Lyon

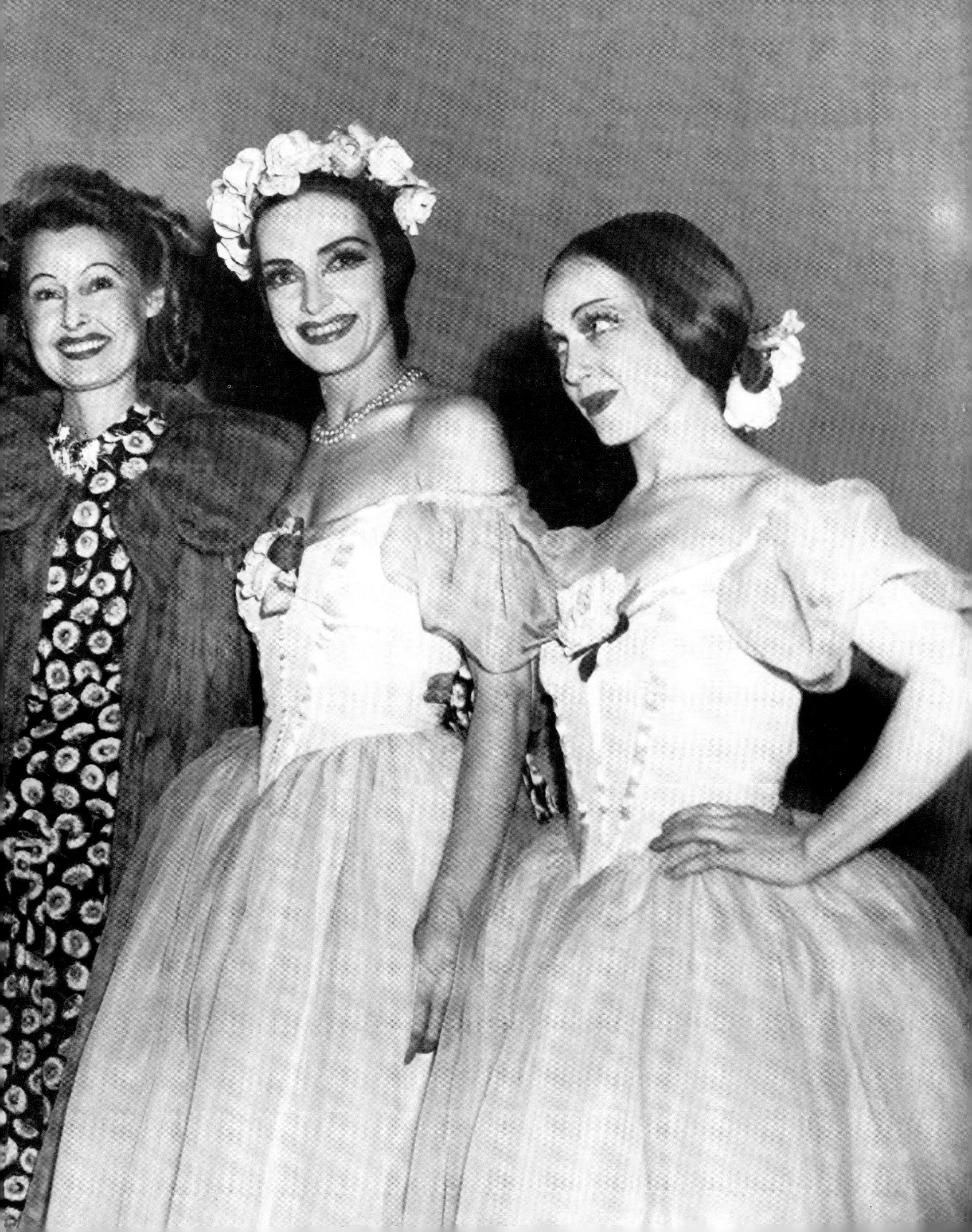

'Some more tea, dear?' How I loved that Moss Hart
skit on Angel Street, how I hated everything else.
New York, 1945

Camille, Metropolitan Opera House, New York, 1945. Cecil Beaton did the decor and costumes, but no bed for Camille to die on, just a window sill – rather stupid. Alicia was divine

In line for ballet tickets in the *Seven Lively Arts* sketch at the Ziegfield Theatre, 1945. Bea Lillie was outrageous, and so was Billy Rose, but in quite a different way: a rose full of thorns

THE GREAT WHITE WAY

Rehearsing for *Seven Lively Arts*, 1945

Meeting Tamara Toumanova from the train in
Montreal, Canada, 1945. No wonder the Redcap is
smiling!

Summer stock, *Blithe Spirit*, USA, 1946. Lilian
Harvey was divine. I don't think 'The Master' would
have said the same about me

Camille. Garbo and Taylor? No! Markova and Dolin.
America, 1947

Bronislava Nijinska's lovely ballet for these two rather lovely looking dancers. No need to name *them*, but the ballet is *The Beloved One*, 1948

above *The Sleeping Beauty*, our first performance of this ballet in 1948 at the Royal Opera House, Covent Garden. Alicia Markova and me in the vision scene

left With Alicia Markova in the second act of *Giselle*, at the Royal Opera House, Covent Garden, 1948

'Double Exposure', a fine Gordon Anthony photo, 1948

right 'Well, Sir Anton, you can't behave like *this* any more!'

A very fine photograph by Gordon Anthony, and what he wrote on the back of it in 1980

Alicia Markova and I arrive at Honolulu in 1948.
What a lei!

right   Happy days, me and Alicia Markova in
Kingston, Jamaica, 1950

Johannesburg, 1949. I was introduced to the
chief African dancer as 'the greatest dancer in the
world'. Like an explosion, he yelled, 'No, *I* am.'

She sang like a bird, the most glorious voice, never forgotten: Jose
Collins, 1949

Tuesday:

TEMPLE BAR 4343

SAVOY HOTEL,
LONDON.

1932

Pat darling –
You were brilliant
I am so proud of you,
I loved every minute
it and your
superb performance
Bless you darling
& thank you –
Jose

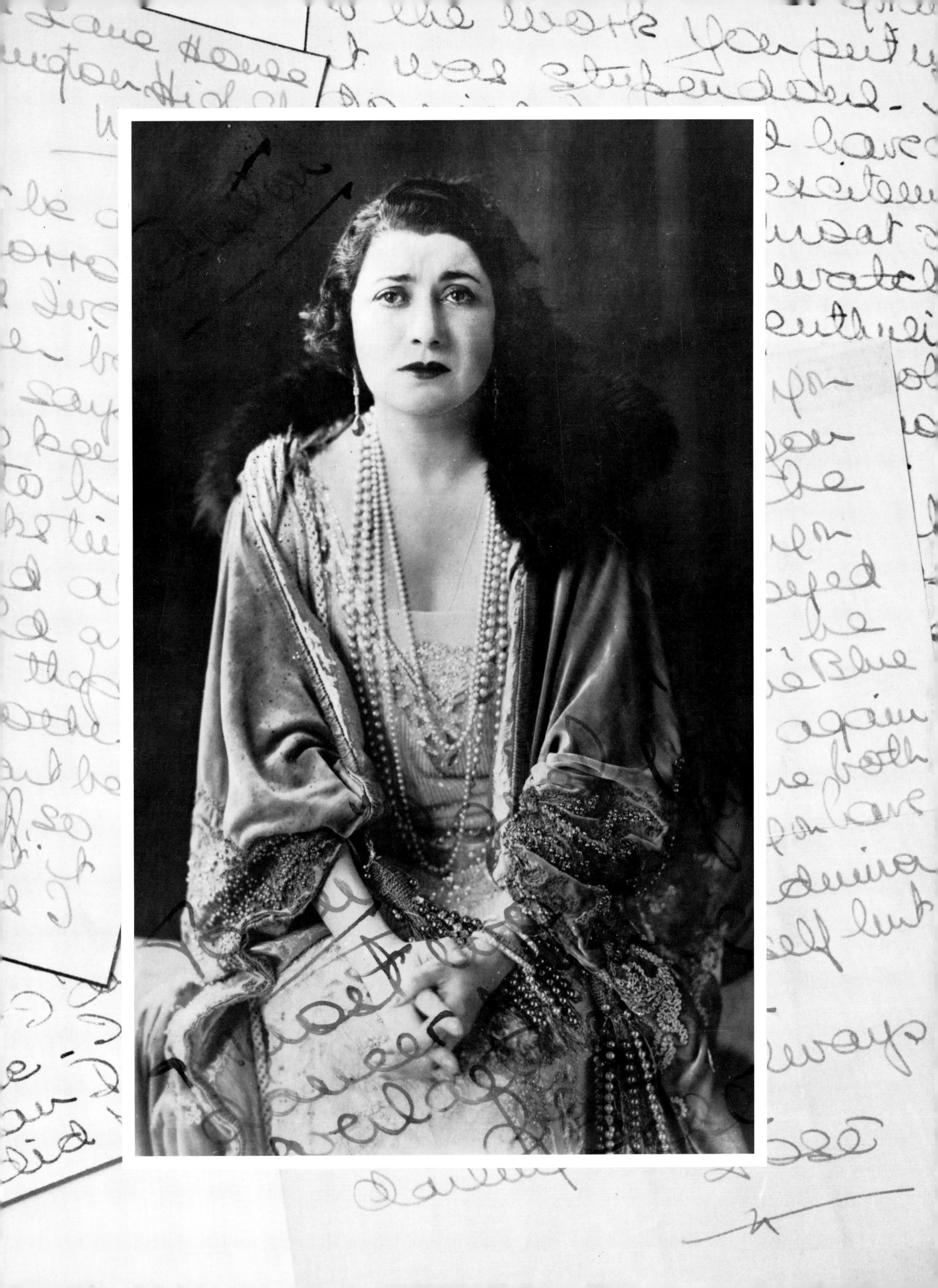

MAKING
BALLET AND
SPENDING MONEY

St George, or me in a blonde wig and armour. Very uncomfortable, but I look like a shining knight. I played *Where the Rainbow Ends* every Christmas from 1949 to 1960, breaking Pauline Chase's record as Peter Pan

Where the Rainbow Ends, Stoll
Theatre, London, 1950

My mother, 1950

Carrying Vaslav Nijinsky to his initial resting place, with Serge Lifar,
Frederick Ashton, and Michael Somes, 1950. Later his remains were
transferred to Père Lachaise to lie next to Madame Vestris, and one day,
to Serge Lifar

above Now, who am I looking back at when I should have been looking at Gracie Fields and Sophie Tucker? Capri, 1951

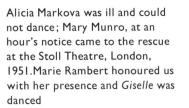

Alicia Markova was ill and could not dance; Mary Munro, at an hour's notice came to the rescue at the Stoll Theatre, London, 1951. Marie Rambert honoured us with her presence and *Giselle* was danced

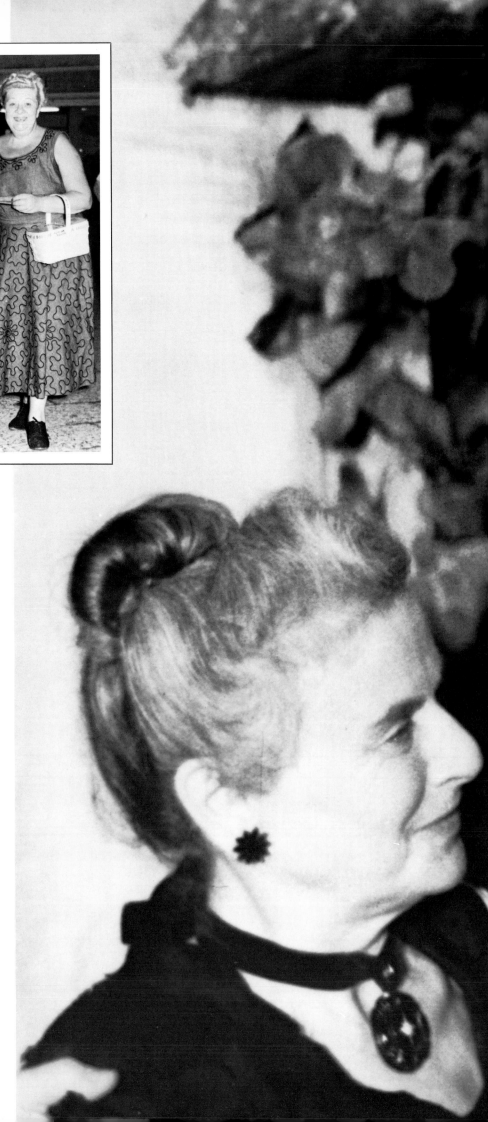

left   Making up for *Petrushka*, London, 1952   *above*   In casual mood at the Royal Festival Hall, 1953

April 9th.

My Dear Pat,

Thank you for your two cables, the first one sweet, the second fairly irritating.

As you may remember in my original scheme for the ballet the hero was to be a policeman who dominated the whole action. This was changed because John considered that a sailor's costume would be more becoming. Now you and Jack Carter and persumably himself wish him to be promoted to a midshipman. If we allow this sort of nonsense to go on he will be a full Admiral before we get to Madrid.

It obviously hasn't struck any of you that a midshipman in the Royal Navy does not in peacetime wear uniform ashore, unless of course he is on official business or about to attend a Levee or an investiture. He might of course be going to receive a V.C. for untold gallantry in his picket boat but this would mean I fear reconstructing the whole story.

If he wishes to dance dressed in a tweed coat and grey flannel bags he can most certainly be a midshipman, in which case I suggest that Andre Prokovski plays the sailor and dances the hornpipe and the two love themes.

I hasten to affirm my opinion that the 'Square Rig' of an ordinary seaman is the most becoming costume in our English tradition, much more so than the American 'Gob' who may have looked attractive in 'Fancy Free' etc: but in real life is diminished by the neccessity of wearing rimless glasses on account of the majority of the American Navy being myopic.

I would suggest that he settles for a well cut Ordinary Seamen's 'Tiddley' suit, very tightly fitting and calculated to emphasise all the fascinating curves etc: of the male physique.

I am only dimly pleased that Jack Carter and Gordon Jacob are delighted with the completed score, because until the 'Delinquents' 'The Schoolgirl's Entrance' and the new theme for the Finale arrive the score will not be complete at all.

Please encourage dear Jack Carter to think out every alluring idea he can for the choreography and the spirit of 'London Morning' without - repeat without altering characterization.

We miss you both very very much. Give my love to John and tell him to keep his rosebud mouth shut, get on with his lissom turns and not devote too much attention to his appearance which will be perfectly charming whatever he wears. You may also give him my slightly exasperated love.

Expect me, articulate and in full spate on the Seventh of May.

Love

+ + +

Noel Coward, 'The Master' never put the year, so why should I?

left 'The Master', with that wicked look

Brigitta, Vera Zorina. There is so much I could say –
all lovely things

'London Morning' with Toni Lander, Louis Godfrey,
Janet Minty, Anita Landa, Pamela Hart, Belinda
Wright, John Gilpin, Michael Hogan, me, Andre
Prokovsky, Marilyn Burr, Vassili Trunov, Deidre
O'Connor, all at the Royal Festival Hall

MAKING BALLET AND SPENDING MONEY

Lilian Harvey

To my Pat
I love you
from
Tallulah

The boy on the left should have been looking at the
beautiful Lubov Tchernicheva. Monte Carlo, 1954

right Galina Ulanova, dancing in the first season of
the Bolshoi Ballet, London, 1957

The Café de Paris, 1957. Only after supper did La
Callas tell me why she chose this famous supper
cabaret: 'I was offered £1,000 a week to come here
and sing.'
Left to right Monsieur Menighini, Wendy Toye, me,
Maria Callas, John Gilpin, Anna Ricarda

MAKING BALLET AND SPENDING MONEY

The first performance of *Variations for Four*, Royal Festival Hall, 5 September, 1957
Left to right   Louis Godfrey, Andre Prokovsky, John Gilpin, Fleming Flindt

Yvette Chauvire as Juliet

My last *Giselle*, September, 1959,
with the great Yvette Chauvire

To Arthur D

with infinite gratitude

above   A happy Atlantic crossing,
SS *France*, 1963, with Nadia
Nerina-Gordon

above left   Keenan, my dresser,
valet, chauffeur and friend, 1926–60.
He's retired now, of course

Miss Ruth St Denis – incomparable

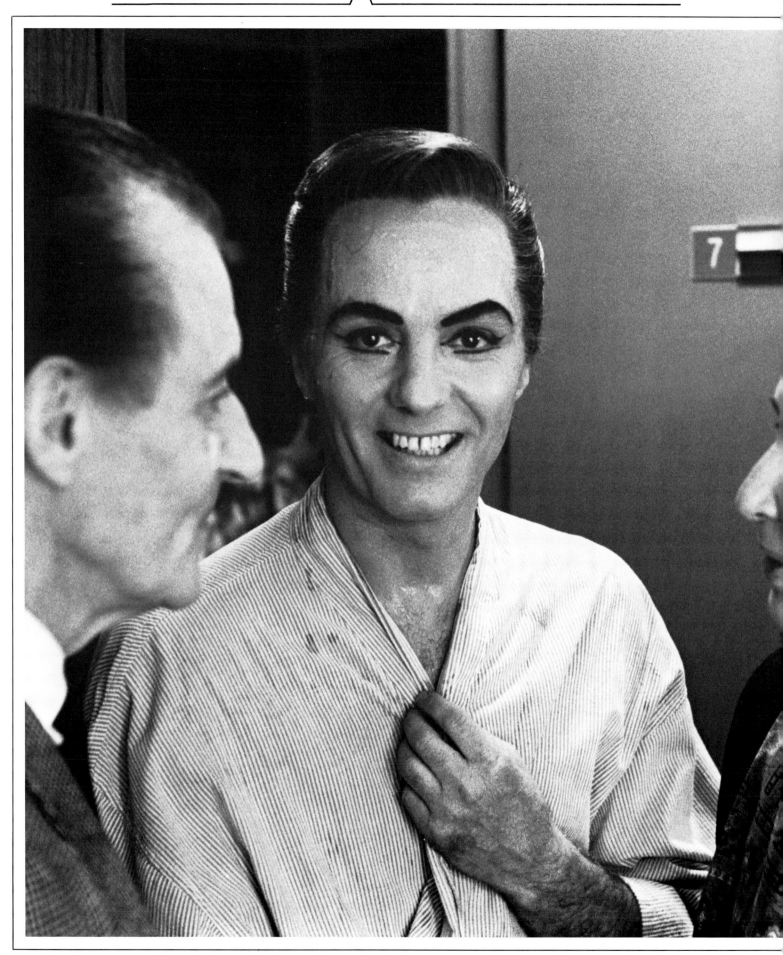

To dean Anton Dolin from his old
friend I Stravinsky
and Vera
Hollywood 1966

Igor Stravinsky and his wife; we first met in Paris when I was on my way
to join the Diaghilev Ballet in 1924

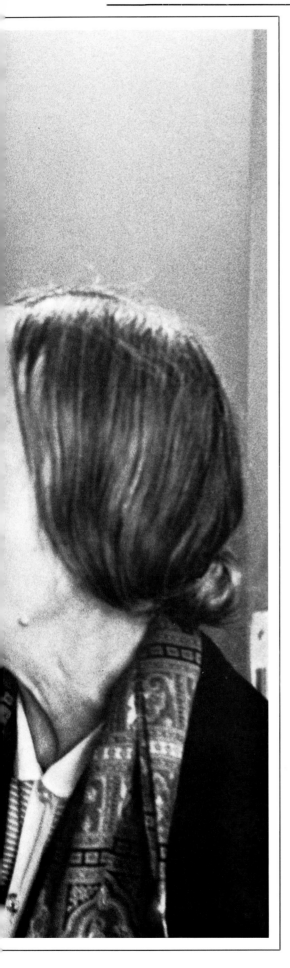

Poking my nose in looking at John Gilpin and Olga Spessiva after a
performance of *Giselle*, Gilpin's first in New York, 1965, and the first
time the divine Olga had ever seen it from the audience

below Capezio asked me if they could use my ballet shoe for an advertisement. I like the result

When Dolin danced a devilishly brilliant Bluebeard, this is the ballet shoe he wore. It was Capezio's privilege to create this black and silver ballet shoe for Anton Dolin, a superb Bluebeard, and a superb craftsman. Capezio's been dancing since 1887.

left Ulanova and me at Nadia Nerina-Gordon's elegant birthday party for Arnold Haskell at the Ritz Hotel, 1972

MAKING BALLET AND SPENDING MONEY

below This is Josephine Baker at her chateau in the
Dordogne with me and Jean Myrio, husband of my
lovely Desha

right Who is the prettiest – me, Ruth Page or John
Gilpin? St Tropez, 1970

With a friend escorting Bluebellaline (Lady Hicks), to Evelyn Laye's 70th birthday tribute luncheon, at the Savoy Hotel, 10 July, 1970.

I have known her since my first appearance as Peter, The Black Cat, in 1916, when she looked after a small and rather frightened young actor

The 35th Gala Anniversary of American Ballet Theatre, in New York, 1975.
Front row Jerome Robbins, Leon Danielin, Karen Conrad, me, Irina Baronova, Lucia Chase, Natalia Makarova, Hugh Laing, Nora Kaye.
Behind Oliver Smith.   *Right* Anthony Tudor

above   Herod in Lindsay Kemp's extravaganza, *Salome*. Evelyn Laye was
horrified at the audacity of it: 'most unprofessional, thinking you can
learn it in ten days. . . .' I did, though

left   Getting older, no wiser – but still imposing. Toronto, 1976

A master class at the Richard France Ballet School in Tucson, Arizona, 1977. I had a lovely holiday right out in the desert with two very dear friends, Enid and Brent Orcutt

right   Not as young as we were, but a lot of nobility and class

What, no shoes, Kevin! Very stupid of you. Kevin Haigen rehearsing *Le Train Bleu*, Hamburg, 1978

What an acrobat and what a dancer!

This is Fidel Castro, friend and admirer of Alicia Alonso. We listened to him for twenty-five minutes at Havana in November, 1978. Surrounding Alonso is her company

A great tribute to a great artiste, the 35th anniversary in 1978 of Alicia Alonso's first *Giselle*. I crowned her with a laurel head-dress, and with her partner, Jorge Esquival, led her forward as I had done that time in 1943 at the Metropolitan Opera House in New York. Now it was *Giselle* in Havana, Cuba

MAKING BALLET AND SPENDING MONEY

My one-man show *Conversations*, Tokyo, 1978

MAKING BALLET AND SPENDING MONEY

A naughty, but most enjoyable *pas de quatre* in Tokyo, 1979. Peter Breuer, Cyril Atanassov, Vladimir Vasiliev and James Urbain. I think the girls were *quite* amused

Cecchetti and the lovely Karsavina (Carla Fracci) do not seem to be talking to each other, on the set of the *Nijinsky* movie. This and the next photograph were taken at the Arts Educational School, Tring. The studios were chosen by Herbert Ross and Nora Kaye

left   Me *as* Enrico Cecchetti *as* The Charlatan in the movie *Nijinsky*, a two hour make-up job. London, 1979

My *Giselle* television talk with Olga Spessiva helped by the presence of John Gilpin, of whom Olga was so fond, at the Tolstoy Foundation in New York State, 1979

This is Dick Cavett talking to me on two half-hour
TV shows on 13 and 14 October, 1980. Shown coast
to coast, they were seen by millions throughout the
USA

Rehearsing *The Romantic Era*, with Alicia Alonso, Mexico, 1980

MAKING BALLET AND SPENDING MONEY

left Dearest Lilian, who could ever forget you. Lilian Gish gave me this at the Ritz Hotel, London, 1980

below The American Ballet Theatre's 40th anniversary, April, 1980, at the Metropolitan Opera House. Two happy people – Irina Baronova and me

Looking very majestic in his livery, my friend William Tallon, but not as majestic as our beloved Queen Elizabeth The Queen Mother, accompanied by three of her grandchildren, Prince Edward, Viscount Linley and Lady Sarah Armstrong-Jones, at the gates of Clarence House on the happy occasion of Her Majesty's 79th birthday, 4 August, 1979

Evelyn Laye, CBE, otherwise known as Boo: my long time, most beloved friend since 1912 at our dancing class in Brighton with Grace and Lily Cone

Ginette Spanier. We danced together at the 50–50 Club, Wardour Street, in 1925. Her French mother was far from amused – 'foxtrotting with a *ballet* dancer!'

MAKING BALLET AND SPENDING MONEY

My second and my last dance with Margot Fonteyn.
God, how nervous I was! The Royal Academy of
Dancing dinner at the Royal Garden Hotel,
2 January, 1981

PICTURE CREDITS

All the photographs in this book are taken from the Dolin Collection.
The author, compiler and publisher are particularly grateful to the
following for their assistance:

Gordon Anthony
Constantine
Mike Davis Studios
Marcel Fugère
Bob Golby
Thomas Kaiser
Louis Klemantaski
Kaiser
Tom Lucy

Ross Macgibbon
Jack Mitchell
Paramount
Louis Peres
Rimis
Maurice Seymour
Thames Television
Tokyo Ballet Company

Left to right My sister-in-law Louie, my brother
Anthony, Beryl Grey, Alicia Markova, my niece
Susanne, Maris Liepa, Me, my nephew Phillip,
Wayne Sleep, Princess Antoinette of Monaco, John
Gilpin, Florence Desmond, Jessie Mathews,
Anthony Dowell, Antoinette Sibley and Ninette de
Valois.

What a day! 5 April 1978. Thank you, Eamonn